Free Verse Editions
Edited by Jon Thompson

CIVIL TWILIGHT

Giles Goodland

Parlor Press
Anderson, South Carolina
www.parlorpress.com

Parlor Press LLC, Anderson, South Carolina, 29621

Printed in the United States of America
S A N: 2 5 4 - 8 8 7 9

Library of Congress Cataloging-in-Publication Data

Names: Goodland, Giles, 1964- author.
Title: Civil twilight / Giles Goodland.
Description: Anderson, South Carolina : Parlor Press, [2022] | Series: Free verse editions | Summary: "Civil Twilight explores the tensions between social roles (work, parenthood, commuting) with the savagery and boundlessness of language itself"-- Provided by publisher.
Identifiers: LCCN 2021038379 (print) | LCCN 2021038380 (ebook) | ISBN 9781643172736 (paperback) | ISBN 9781643172743 (pdf) | ISBN 9781643172750 (epub)
Subjects: LCGFT: Poetry.
Classification: LCC PR6057.O54 C58 2022 (print) | LCC PR6057.O54 (ebook) | DDC 821/.914--dc23
LC record available at https://lccn.loc.gov/2021038379
LC ebook record available at https://lccn.loc.gov/2021038380

978-1-64317-273-6 (paperback)
978-1-64317-274-3 (pdf)
978-1-64317-275-0 (ePub)

1 2 3 4 5

Cover photo by Frankie Lopez on Unsplash.
Cover design by David Blakesley.

Parlor Press, LLC is an independent publisher of scholarly and trade titles in print and multimedia formats. This book is available in paperback and ebook formats from Parlor Press on the World Wide Web at http://www.parlorpress.com or through online and brick-and-mortar bookstores. For submission information or to find out about Parlor Press publications, write to Parlor Press, 3015 Brackenberry Drive, Anderson, South Carolina, 29621, or email editor@parlorpress.com.

In memory of Mahmud Kianush: friend, neighbour, poet.

Contents

Civil Twilight

The Language

The gravel slipping under the car, the train gathering purpose, shrapnel from a shattered rainbow, the house that name built, a man singing his son an unidentifiable song as he pushes him on a swing, the dual in individual, trees indexical and brightening towards the east, the suicides calling from the sea, conversations with the wind, what words talk about when we're not using them, a raft of measures, the knowledge that sucks the telephones black, all the contractions of I to is, fixed beliefs that when interrogated belong to no one, new exploratory drillings to find words under the icecap, tongue deadening against meat, mist in translation, the wind's way home that names itself harder, the hole in the self, the one the words fell from, matter's irresolution, fissure of imaginable lament collapsing under the weight of its signs, cigarette smoke from the crack in a car window, the explaining doll, the wolves from the forest of symbols that only pause at the suburban edge, their eyes walk light onto the grass, what a map contains if it is a map of language, capital of cloud, behind the lyric, older than state, something that animals would not have thought, the never-weeded corner in the dust at the end of the eye, the object: the stone, that upon which we tread, retread, the map of your failures, an open wound that makes insides apparent, a cluttered and deep-basemented house, in which we bark our shins trying to find what may be useful to say, an alphabet marching through the dark, selves sifting inside, a sieve for a soul (the sound releases its sense, glucose into brain), that which explains itself by its name, of stars, always negotiable, if the stars explode, ignore them since it is in their nature, but always let us hear first what they have to say.

The Wren

Listen, season's myrrhy rhythm thm thm.
A flight in half-light, a wren, moth-
featured, lights upon the last leaf's flame.
Look through the lenses of its
eyes to wrench yourself inside,
beak divides world into food
and threat. Threats into
immediate and mediate. In a
split world, sift for gold or
solder through wasp-drift, observe
the bees' tendency of blooms
the pondering fruits, off-drift
think rapidly, dust the light, jerk back there,
stitch here, among the immaterial, mere
thoughts, effusive clouds
call from them little notes of what. Name.
To shadow in a light-shaft dance, undance.
Who would think to correct a song
or find in flight something wrong.
Its only mistake is to be overseen.
Like a fit answer that returns
fly through holes to present messages.

Košava

Each wind in this country is named for
the noise it makes in the trees.
Today through the People's Park the Košava bursts
as I sit in the glass-walled café at the centre.
A man pushes a piled shopping-cart of crates
of soft drinks across the Narodna Bašta
and suddenly the wind upsets them all
in furious colour and fizz. The fountain tilts
everything that can wave waves
the air-drunk trees tip, the Cyrillic
death-notices flap against the trunks.
To my eyes every thing has the appearance of
the thing that it is, and even this strong wind
fails to quite dislodge the image of tree that half-
buckles, its roots holding, as a few young
leaves stream away, such loss being the cost
of representation, accounted for
in the sense that the trees overproduce
leaves in anticipation of loss, and once the
crisis-point passes, they will stand
more lightly tree-like than before, but does
the streaking leaf remain a part of the tree
or is it only in me its image races
until I stalk it inside a poem:
the streaming never, the loose leaf,
metonym of eternity never
still enough to tell. And is that a bird
in the despite, against the rush, undistressedly
notating? It is unseen, unseeable
and the other leaves, the ones that remain,
turn their paler undersides, making the trees
appear to be rushing from the scene.
About us blow the names of things, I sit
feeling dislodged from the great tree of name
and falling, since there is nothing to do but fall.

Twilight of the Twigs

Travel through the changing language
disturbing here a leaf or twig
or delineating a grove in a storm's
agitation (to paraphrase Johnson)
upon the Thames a certain glow persists
but largely it is the dark you push
through the febrile glass of the train
beyond the reflections you still see
the pivotal towers. Everyone is
sleeping—it occurs to you
you have to wake just to witness that which
you have seen thousands of times.
But each time the light fell
differently. Each lit twig
that spun away from you contained
and withheld the next spring's leaves.

The Drive Home

There is sand still in our hair
a few sea-querned pebbles tucked in
the car's door-pockets, among other
depositions of this holiday's last leg.
The kids sleep like crated coke bottles.
All day they'd seemed unaware
you were ill, and driving past midnight
north from the coast needle on red it feels
as if I am untwisting us, and we could fizzle
out long after you nod at the turns,
pain-killers having wrapped you in that white
tissue I think is sleep, at least a silence
that shows pain has ebbed. We don't
know what's wrong with you yet and have
been driving like this, it seems, for days.
Climbing the valley with this sense of
how fragilely the car's sleepers depend
from my hands, a high-beamed stag lifts its
interrupted face, and bounds a fence.
I cry out and you respond: you too, in
or out of sleep, had seen it. That stag for
your sickness, outleaping pain, now lost
in the tangle our light makes of woods,
replacing them with fields, houses, the petrol
station's empty kiosk, empty carbs, vending
machine's museum-displays, then motorway-
trance, slip and exit roads. We lift the children into
the unlit hall. Half woken, they reach
their arms around our necks and try to cling.

Thread

A door opens in the grass called
uncaused crow, called derisively awkward.
The crow causes the upstart hare
the storm-cloud ascends its stairway
a run-dry pond stirs up a leaf.

We've been carrying the corpse of time for
so long he feels heavy, but it is critical that we
do not stop to put him down.

Somewhere on the hill there's a great view of
the city but as it's late summer we
trespass the golf-course before we can see over
the brash clamour of bramble-fuzz.

Look through the brow, feel
reminded and abstract, earth falls from
the feet first
the air is crossed by winged figures,
we pinch ourselves to check if time's still dead.

That plane in the hazeless sky also is,
observe, caught in its own thread.

Coal

Incendiary and petrified,
all stone should be like you.
Coal, you are the colour of a river at dusk.
I looked up and saw a hundred
rooks in one tree and as I walked under them
they flew away and
coal you are like those rooks as well,
they have flown to the next tree ahead of me.
Coal, are you listening?
Or are they blackbirds? They sound like
coal splintered with a hammer.
I think you have always been my friend.
I'm almost weeping as I say this:
as I walk I see a hospital on the hill.
It is burning electricity, people inside
blacken and grow hard. If you are
death is it so bad to be dead?
You are not inert, I turn you to the light,
you shine with diamond teratomas.
Coal, I am descended from a long line
of smoke. When I was fourteen I
sold you under my father's office.
It was the day before the Xmas break,
people came in their lunchtime.
They would push coins into my palm:
keep it, they would say, and I looked
at the high window over the yard. To hold
you cold coal is to know how deeply
we have dug. Coal, my car will bore
through the night. You are base, we
are superstructure. I don't think
you were ever a tree. I look into you and see
compressed dragon. If you ever swayed
in the wind and lifted your head to the sun
and ached for water you can have
no memory, we must imagine you

as all of the dead languages we use.
They are bedrock, we burn them when we speak.
Coal, I am walking away from you
trying to find my car. It is
somewhere dark, bedded in the night.

The Start of the Question

Moon's thumb-ridge on mist.
The day's glass rains down as appearance.

Two swans just far
enough apart for their
wings to not touch, rush, impress
their wing-prints on canal-water.

The dissident thrushes,
the cloud's downfall at my feet:
impatient for language to start, the gulls
deride and yaw in return,

but here are my prints on the paving.

When I get home it is as if none of
this is there in a sense that
matters. There've been too many
quests, too few questions.

The Pond

Pond. Moonrise. Trees
and domed behind them
night's uncertain premise:
if it is not the start it
must be the end of the day.
The mushroom lifts its veil
signs the protocols of
acting in the world.
The birds anticipate
light by singing for it.

Gravity

Throned on the slide
when I told him what pulled
him down, he repeated
'grabbity'. The word allows
some slippage, so at the slide-
foot he collects himself
and I climb him up again. He's short
or I'm tall enough to hold his arms
even to the top. The children
read us inside them, and
we have in us a small demon
converting thought to action,
grabbing, under a cloud-asterisk
made of three crossing jet-
trails, a stupefied cloud.

Words are frames. I was taught this.
Teachers were taught, stretching
in a line to Plato or mute unnamed
plateaux upon which buildings
open abstractly, and light through the grove
shone in on those who spoke
of that which issued from the wide wise earth.

The air piles up. This happened years ago,
I'm mourning the childhoods of my children.
Smile up on the cloud, it is full of years

and pushes into time, the
peculiar light catching in his hair.
Between fork and spoke, we travel light
until our long weights pull us down.

At Kilve

Grey simmer over the bay.
The muscled waves by crook of arm
fold the mountain, raise the crust
wash cuttlebones. White tongues
clatter, speechless in down-surge.

Notebooks fill with the sea's sense-archive
an ounce of ocean in each eye becomes
self of the perceiving sieve.

A massing of geese, shankily
falling over themselves, cranes,
shovelbeaks: upright citizens
laughing away a reign of terror.

The sun king sinks under the weight
of state, his head of enormous hair,
foamed arms unravelling.

The sea expounds its idea of storm
upon England's idea of a coast,

pierces the crab's crevice-device
as if self is unsafe inside its shell.
We make what land we can: not in
hell, but nor are we out of it.

On Numinosity

The leaves swept us aside and
this world was none other than
beamed into us, N asking how can
He sit in the clouds and not fall through?
S corrects her, and correcting him
I tell her whether I think God might exist
but cannot bring myself to say
definitively He is the left over,
both instigator and ruin
the toy left by the stair-gate
but anyway somehow existing
where we are not in the sense that
nothing sits between matter, nothing
is all powerful, we shake apart from this,
insects sing in to the room but
only the most powerful nothing can
not fall through cloud, but I've confused
myself, the moon slams open its
door to show its final reductio
the eye loosens what we judge to be
dream as mountains clamp their teeth
and the forecast is beyond bleak,
and under the white plains stored
in narrow-necked jars are
the scrolls that will translate us:
the invalid, the residual contracts.

War

The war starts peacefully
the downed arm of the helmeted airman
sleeps, the moon sleeps on the brow, mind
acts upon sight, events take

we are as if waiting for the film to start
but cross the marshes
stamp joy into these faces

the second stores bullets and releases them
they range forward, displace,
are agents of chance upon the rose
lip, the shaved cheek.

The bullets' bee-tenderness is
single-minded in seeking dark, from
origin's groin to point of spray
it burrows against its own seed.

The sinewed dead stumble up and cannot
blink into their eyes how
the exit is marked in red.
The projectionist's door is locked.

We, the audience, had not noticed
smoke fill the whole space
until the lights come back.

Feel between ridges
a tiredness seep in the wind.
The airman is now air.

Unspoken

N always reads 'saw' as 'was'.
She leans out of bed to see
that the rats have moved into the garden.
Today I'll run behind her on the pavement
my hand above the saddle telling her
I'm holding tight: that inch of air will be
the white space of a lie. Not yet:
I step into the road gripping her
handlebar like an eager puppy's collar.
The park ahead will be full of footballers
massing towards some distant shimmer
that will prove when we get close to be
the pressing arguments of flesh. She
stretches a long word into that
sea-like light, sawing
at the wastes where the trees stand
for something like a question.
On a bench I'll try to sort dream
from memory as if it matters which
is more real, since even among
damp litter and noise a tree can
suspend these yellow explosions that
contain the reactionary blackbirds
and a white fog of body, not
momentarily but engaging
and returning a moon-derived stare, each leaf
a judgement to cast aside. I watch her
from time-frame to climbing
frame, over stretches of feel, of
handled sense. She is asking, is God
made out of cloud. Concerning
the evening sky the gathering spectres will
open under the thunder, and close.

Horse

The geese call suggesting
our sky has been crossed
by a limitless word, falling.

Most of all, suggesting the horse's mass,
its continent chewing. Night stacks
inside it. Soon it will shift to
the counter-edge of the field, lift it
with its bone teeth and pull it in.

Streetlights come on, snowflakes
dance like summer midges.
The house spills light, the horse shadow.
The air is hungry, barks
a chained dog. Mopeds tut
to each other. Further, a police car

wows. The birds creak like sleep-
crusted springs, one-leggedly
sleepy. The horse sleeps standing.
And further, something larger
changes gear: bus, planet, word.

Walpole Park

The playground swing ground to a halt.
There were the birds' phatic songs.
We sat and drank hot chocolate.
A squirrel came forward, I had popcorn
left in my bag. It took a piece
delicate-fingeredly turning it:
a jeweller assaying for flaws.

Eyes half closed, not
opening my book, I watched their,
the children's, branchings, their strung
sinuosity. Each turn will guide them
towards a different set of cubicles
some might lead them
to a place like this, where I am not.

I held their scuffed school-bags
they hid-and-sought until
they found a blue metal box in the bushes
and dragged it to me, small fingers
clasped, and I told them what
it was. It was a rat-trap.

I checked back through my voluminous
learning. Put it where you found it.
They became like the small
birds on the grass finding their voices,
finding they are not so small.

Hate

Even love hates you S said to his
sister as we walked back from the pool.
I thought if they were good I would buy them
some chocolate, I thought of its slabby
quality of compliance, but did not.
Even the birds and the mice, they hate you,
he said, all those you thought were your friends,
the rain and the sun hate you also.
The language, the air, the sound of your
own voice, they all hate you, there is
nothing in the universe that does not
order itself into hate when it considers
you, your own toes and hair and face
hate you, why can't you see how things
just choke up when you walk past them.
And N walked on, sulky because she'd
not learnt to dive: she knew what her body
had to do but posed on the pool edge and
fell in, n-shaped, repeatedly. There were no
buses so we walked home tired through
an exuberant after-dusk raininess,
hurrying to make dinner through the park
of old flaring sunlights, the insular obstinate
remain that edges the lost farmsteads.
Now it is bare streets up to Woodfield Road.
Nearing home he asks her, are we friends?

Felling

Tried to move out from the bay, but
there were bollards over the road
a set of lights that were not there an hour before.
A man was in the beech, harnessed,
disassembling it a limb at a time.

It was like the kind of haircut where
you are rooted in the chair and the barber
does not stop at the scalp.
In the course of a deferred thought,

I watched a squirrel cross the verge,
its tentative, liquid start-stop,
its threat-response, its stop-
turn to pick up what looked
like an apple-core
then half way up an opposite tree, in
the branches, eating,
another branch came down.

Stacked planes
waited to collapse back into the thoughts
they were, their shadows
mine. A short wind puffed round the
corner, a hurled-up leaf.

He came to me and I lowered my window.
He explained that the lights depended on
sensors and I had not moved my car
close enough for the lights to change.
Assuming that I want to go anywhere.

No Ideas

For Mahmud

No day but in the eyes of a boy
balancing on the line of
paving that tightropes
him to school. No moment
but inside the cat whose
eyes sunder the territory. Ideas
crack from surfaces, the light
hinges from a cloud. A rain
bow in the drain,
a bird speaks its bright notion,
in its beak it cannot be
song, it bears too much
that has just this side of
occurred: the derivative rain,
opposing clouds crusted
over the London planes
the beeches and horse-chestnut:
nothing without its idea is
whole. We meet for coffee and
talk overflows the table and
notions flood the street. You are
old, I saw the wind push past you
as it rushed for the next uprising
in the trees, and you nearly
fell. Child is running to
the next day, making up
time, eyes ahead, like whatever
floats on wind there has no idea but in
hinge, no laughter but in
night no nights but in bars
there are no bars but in songs
we are not the children we
were but when we were children
neither were we then those
children. I see the leaves over
take you on your way home.
He is light. You are light.

Mitten

In the changing-room corner he
pulls on a grey sock, and then a leg-
brace. One testicle lolls, the way he
moves suggests pain. I leave after him,
find him struggling
to work out the exit, the knob you have
to press. I unlock my bike
think about the next thing in my day
catch up with him past the steps.
He has dropped his wet swimming shorts,
I pick them up (leaving their
grey shadow on the paving) and pass
them to him as I cycle, then stop

to watch him walk
painfully round a corner stop for
a moment, stoop to pick
up a child's mitten from the ground
and place it on a low tree
stump and move on.

Surfaces

The wind sharpens against the road
the blood mills in the finger
the animals square in the sun

antique insects dip and skim
piece together the moon, evidence
spoken through the night. The witnesses
are credible, but the judge sleeps.

We want all the words at the
same time, we want no words, no
time, just language's long rain.

Cellophane

As the streetlights woke slowly runners
dissolved in the park and rain
worked through my cycle-jacket. A woman
with a red umbrella
was talking to her dog, which was
ignoring her, and I did not understand
that she had not seen me until I
could not stop, and having no bell
I shouted to warn her. I had in
my basket a bunch of lilies I'd bought
at the station for 90p (reduced),
the cellophane wrapping of which
brushed her and she let out that
vocal, non-verbal noise of disgust
people make some times, pure
expression, but I don't see her face
nor she mine and then we are gone.

Quoth the Sea

Beware my kiss among the seaweed stalks
the bone-lace wave
rubbishing among the pools
the whale who booms in to
bone-bound muscle.

We imagine and then enter it
and fashion the verb into
rim of the glistering forgotten.
Silence is immeasured until
pointed by tide-mud braillings.
I watch the rocks weather your shoes.
This we are sinking in is not sand, not
sad as silk tears on the swell,
world-clogged water of the eye flows.

The seal-swarming
wave-tilt at breakwater
addresses the stuff of waves, casts aside
handshakes. Licit strong bonds govern
us but pulled also by underchains, ids,
the sea has a degree in silence
turns obsequiously
in pragmatic movements, loosening
where language rips other language
apart is where language starts.

A River

Edge the pain towards the child:
a matter of years. Nevertheless
snow fades upon so much that is laid,
the endless stretched-out plans.

They hit us with small fists and we fix them
into beds as if to apply this to life.
We're afraid they'll come out indifferent
as if there was ever a coherent child
or a unified fly

the lung inversely tree hangs
between early morning's porch-
light, shows the dim way behind
the steps. Blank leaderless rain falls on us
as we wait for human shapes.

Lost dogs run before they melt, before
light splotches the road and
fragments of conversation pace at path-foot.

When the road is quiet you hear
the storm-drain whisper.
The blush in that
field grows,
the truer lie bends in

the catch the moon is sky to
kindles, it seems objects are
river of inside, inspection, that silts
her wrists and wraps her self in ribbands.

Deep Sea

Conscious glint of ocean at daybreak
kelp forests retrace, retract
destroyers grind the seabed

past the gently shelving grey
waves are pulses through us.

The sun under the sea is the sun
the sea accepts

a faraway touch-screen responds like steel
doesn't, riveted to no surface.

It's time for the brilliant sharks to clear up

a word on glass feet looks for a home.
It's been walking the underworld for months
and now the island rises steeply.

The horizon seems to curve like
the world, but
open the window in the wave
to see there is no world.

Excess

Woke with smell of matches from downstairs
and the children burning pieces of kitchen
when I come down their faces melt.
To elicit from my tendons a creak of love
they preen at my scalp and find glitter.

I'll divide my DNA, don't think a
poem will survive but perhaps a turn of
phrase. Tell them do no felony, do
harmony. Nitrates leach through groundwater,
generations later the springs bloom green.

Above all the sun stares exactingly
forcing them through homework and dinner
and then television; after that I'm
padding round, tidying up.

The sky fits around the buildings.
At night to write like a musician, improvise
air. For love I would dig past the tender
noses of moles, down where graves
rest like spaceships and bury my head
until amethysts crust inside.

Train in Winter

Snow lodged in tread-marks at a field-edge
exposes the tractor-driver's care for detail.

I'm watching a charcoal
cloud, underlit thinly. Years pass. Couples walk
the aisle of a different carriage.

I feel the deceleration but the platform
may still be some time away.
Looking out to streetlights, a car-showroom
glows inwardly, a house-window is exposed,

a curtain, droplets of people. A sickly
moon leans in. For how long have we not
moved. Lights are passing us but they are

of cars. Groups of orange-clad rail-workers
cluster around floods.
The last train has no body, only bodies.

February Train

Today just a little more light
to see at least the sun's downfall and how
the seams of half-flooded fields part
—in October the oaks had not
exposed their inner nature, the trees of ivy, écorché
lymph-systems above

tractor-tracks, abandoned black-sheathed
bales, dusk-inflected cirrus.

If I do not choose
to sleep, sleep will come upon me.

The pylons lead towards
the down-regions of cloud.
A residential area, a park, inside the park
a playground, alone in
the playground in a bright coat, a child.

Everyone on the train is sneezing
energetically and saying sorry and bless.

Ghost Train

On the way to the graveyard for lunch
I passed the primary-school.

The bees poll-vaulted from lavender-stems.
A fine frass sifted from the yew.
Pollen edged some epitaphs with yellow.

Again the school: hand-holding child-couples
by the railings tested
the closing distances between them.

Three more hours of work. I pushed words around
imagining I could hear the playground
but it was long past pick-up time.

The train was crowded. I closed
my eyes, but could not shut out

the grown children who now sit
across from me with beers and jeer
as we pass fields of ash, winters.

The Floods

Fields turn to mirrors as if silver has always
planed beneath this.
Closely observed dust appears
to be stalked, to sustain
a thin layer between thing and
reflection: lyric over smoke.
The rain in its finery descends. I hear
the storm-drains murmuring but when water
knocks we drown in verdigris.

At the end of the field flakes of gulls
unearth under heavy clouds that
somehow don't fall.

Three swans overfly, their shadows like those
of three bombers, but their reflections
whiter than the cloud, descend.

They hold on their backs
waterdrops, they use their raised wings as sails.
They are the first sailors, they will sail with me.

Train, morning

Greasy sky over Didcot,
steam tufts the river.
The sun picks a way
through bare trees.

Two swans above the Union Canal
unaware of or indifferent to

us, the bottles of us standing
in long metal crates, as the sun
stands them in air, splays their wings,
strips of everything but morning

the valley sumps
into aquifers, nitrogen
suffuses the water-tables.

In order to pick up the lost time
the train grinds to dust the sunlit
arcades. We have all seen them,

many of us have been them,
the people filtering
towards their places of work.

Their palaces, the front façades' full
heights are glazed, the first ones in
trip the strip-lights, and their
cold fingers summon

clear blue lakes that resolve into words,
great undraining seas of work.

Cyclist

It rained so hard that we stood
from our desks and clustered under
the light-well, looking up,

but when it's time to leave work, minutes later,
there's only a whisper in the storm drain,
minted puddles to cycle through, past
the heavy-natured cars
it is the fineness of the day

on the opposite bank the cows reach
down, disturbing the overhanging
dripping alders. The chambers
of their hearts open, the Thames
urges into them. I ding three
times for the blind corner, stand to
pedal hard for the short steep corner, and
stoop to clear the tunnel.

At the station I have time to buy a beer.
Observe above the station roof the peaked
the hard departing clouds.

Stone Mirror

Horses crop over it, wind equivocates.
The thrush naps on it the snail.
The cloud in the glacier moves its arm.
Rain writes its instantly erased history on it

while in the hand of the boy
beside the pond is the pebble he throws
to watch the picture break, the channel
change, the animals turn their educated eyes.

They die where they fall, lichen scabs
the limbs that rolled them here. The boy
sleeps into another dawn's gold sift. Stone's
reflection is deep, the

mirror lets him see through matter's
sleep, to the eyes' future.

Forked Star

The clash of two nothings makes a kind of
motion; bluebell-tremble, thoughtswing.
The fine rain falters, falls
the body sings its dead note.
Stone tells me that bird is angle in shadow
it heaved upon and bird confirms us
as woods spill we make this up and
children affirm it. Time is balled
and thrown, not caught, destructs like
a snowball, construct of us and ice.

We follow the sign of the forked star
apprehend through reason
a tree adjusting in the wind
its monocle, smoothing its hair.

This childhood had a mouth in it
from which a river passed.
Scabs peel to show behind them
pink is new, caterpillar in softening
wrinkle, unwink at us, the light is blue
the imponderable passing from experience
fits until you look closely
and the fact there's no give becomes a
problem, if nothing gives then the sun
would not have space to set in us
it is expedition of the eye
the sifting, continuous, the polyp-like waving
in the air in the hope of catching a mote

there were many visits to the local dump
where we liked to watch
the bright machines of autumn
grab boldly from the skips and metals
drooled from their teeth, and we could see
to destroy is almost benign.

2nd January

Municipal lorries ply from bin to bin.
Light spills from the streets.
A song is made from the gearing and tipping
and occasional shouts of the workmen.
There is plenty in empty bottles
expended rockets
and soiled wipes. Discord in discards.

A plane pushes through cloud, then is
enclosed again, to what extent
is the plane itself
the cloud, the people contained, each one
a cloud. I'd been sleepless

as all night the rough wind
drew in to itself. Thinking about work,
how to shape from it
some engagement, some return

these songs lead eventually to a square
in a town's neglected quarter
in which the untended rose-bushes
still give out a scent that no one
names despair. This too is song
as in expression, as matter
rusts and exalts. Bleeds out
its loss, sings the beautiful air.
Inspire, expire. It is a fine
distinction, which we refine

until the clouds pucker
cumulonimbal plumes,
a dog arches and stools, a final
worker with a black bag and a stick follows
litter trails from the eviscerated bins, whistling.

A Beach

On a beach were curlews and waves.

The waves were a distant fading line
or the earth's curve,
the line of the poem breaking
into smudge, a party of two

as we took ourselves
towards the door in the sand, sand and
run mud. Slate is dead mud, is dead
and of all those tracks that died, slate is
slutch wiped clean, this
unwritten feel that welled towards

the slate beach, and the light was late
and by this enacted the coming
of language into knowledge as if it
was the consciousness of language

the beach manufactured sand for us, we
milled down to where the becoming
sand hurt the eye, waves raked

a hooded infant scowled from his pram
soon he'll be striding downwards
or driving his body deep into others
his expression changed as he saw
before him another small child, gazing back

my words over the grass-like sea
under the blindly making blue went
to catch the wind with my hands

it's all down to the sea, waves
raking, pushing its forms onto the other things.
Arms are not enough, pull them out
the sand is made of light, it falls

the sandcasts lit through, the particles.
I made a sand farm, a sand fair and animals, tiny
gates and bales of sand.
My castle won no prizes, rightly:
It was no castle, it was open and trodden in.

Stand up Paddle Board

We stand on a clear nothing above
a swarm of marble-size jellyfish,
almost water-coloured monads, senseless
and fissile, and then see the larger ones,
severed hands spreading nerve-trails as we learn
balance with the small surges and wakes.
A loose-leaf tea of fish swills at the bottom.

Colour is fig trees, is beach's
demilune, further away than I'd like,
above all, the sky, huge but undermined
by these near-nothings massing
beneath us, until I fall without a splash
and for a few moments it's
like touching trodden grapes, or
between grape and wine, only
feelable with fingertip and ear,
not the palm or the foot. I collect
myself back on the board shipwreck-
fashion, to see my children
are almost dissolving, almost gone.

Nature is green and badly lit, or the sea is.
No one knows days as a whole
only as spirals of weather, holders for
events, steps on a progress towards
haze. It's the last day of the holidays.
The swimmers are melting
my offspring have rounded the bay
but here I am again, walking on water.

Lostmarc'h

Out of the tent, when I reach
up to touch the sheet of mist, it feels warm.
Patches of mud are revealed,
lighten, and the sound of waves
grows. At the dune-edge
the vans are still in dew's
bubble-wrap. The beach is not quite wiped
clean: a few trails, drag-marks.
On a headland I breakfast and watch
the surfers, sealed in black skins,
hold the waves, then drop.

Beneath the ribcaged undersides
of ferns the grains, the alignments.
The dream of a perfect wave
is also pulse, wet-suited
grace, the stones, the old track,
thin clouds, all point.

The sun now breaks over the beach.
Stones in rows and in my palm
an impressed design of sand.

The Waves

It is the summer of the year of the latest crisis,
the news breaks upon the managed
coast of a Mediterranean city.
A goggled 5-year-old runs into a wave
all afternoon. What is it about
the world she is learning? That that there is
always contradiction is cause for
joy, matter is motion, all we touch
either hums or shifts. If it should not it
and we would cease. Time as
sand and time as sea, we are drawn here
despite the plummeting pound, the new low,
are swimmers through media of
water and gravity, of irresolvable suspension
and our will to not sink, to weave
and warp waves' infirmities
as if the marks we leave are
net value, shirt of Nessus, flame.
The clouds build walls out of the ruins of
sea, the gulls assemble for prayer.
Waves seize upon and drag from deckchairs
the belongings: towels, goggles, sun-lotion.

Now I am in them, investigating
their nature by entering upon them
convexing their light-casts as
they form wave-forms, causation's
unlinear swells, each one bluer, taller
until I arm wave level-
headedly and through the goggles come
fish-splinters, shims of ginger-
fingered corals parallel-pointing
fear of evisceration from reefs where
the bred in-the-dark weeds hold sway
under the black rock, unclimbable,
to which I feel willed through choppy waters
and cling before I control my drift
back to the deckchairs, curbed
arena-like to face the heat-
daze, the still running girl.

Swimmers, Pančevo

The swimmers in the brown river dissolve.
A willow's shadows sway on my page.
Regular slow squeak from a see-saw.
A naked 4 year old sits with his father
or grandfather. Two men in shorts
are playing chess under a high-stilted
café, board spread between their knees.
Serbian šah, flowing perhaps from
Sanskrit *chaturanga*, the four soldiers.
The sun does not deter one runner.
On my notebook the shape of each leaf.
A *ciganka* flower-seller passes with a basket.
I've arranged to meet my kids in an hour
at the other end of town. I'll be their guide
for a year or two more, I think, but
meanwhile sit by the side of my thoughts by
the Tamiš' half familiar name, linked
to Thames by language-flow, roots oozing
the trade-routes. From *temeslos,*
Proto-Celtic for darkness. Before that,
Indic and European jostle and merge.
'Roots' seems like a bad metaphor to me.
Origins are dark and irrecoverable.
Perhaps roots, but not from any single tree.
Birds flock from the west and the forest on
the opposite bank holds a man, fishing.
The two swimmers lie on a bench;
they are suddenly old. I get up and walk past
the slow chess game to see who's
winning, and then turn towards
the kids. That evening Z, who grew up
and tall by these banks, tells me this
is the 'day of change', after which you are
not to swim. The light will shorten,
the river rise, the café on stilts be
just a café beside fast-flowing water
the chess-pieces swept back into their days.

Baka's House

Spiders arrive like surveyors,
triangulating the plastic dolls on
the couch and armchair. The wallpaper
loosens. Damp seeps, seeks.

She gives me a tray of keys, one for
each scrapy outhouse and one for
the walled orchard
where the quince-trees spilt
solders among weeds so long-established
they reach over my shoulders
and walking in them I am lost.

Burrs cling to my socks. I feel
a toddler-like bewilderment, then see
a hurt cloud limping towards its horizon
the hen-house hipped on the outhouse,
Baba-Yaga fashion, more sky than slat.

The Day of the Drive

We came out on the other side of the mountain
to find a new church.
The land was flat and wheaty, bony trees
predominated, what was nowhere
close to hunger churned into hunger
but we only consumed road, shrugged past
the shoulder blades of Europe. At some
points heavy rain, thunder, then slowly
a better sky unfolded, the sun cut
into the clouds, treelines ceded to roofs,
hoardings, brief images of those in the fields
when there were fields. The green-gloved
way, the hard shoulder, the soft. Tunnels,
speed traps, chalets, she said it was like the Alps
without the mountains. We parked in a vineyard
and ate the rolls from breakfast, with filched cheese.
Beside me, Z's jaw slackened in sleep.
Then a closed motorway, a diversion, unclear
why or where the road led off under
the autobahn, the satnav recalibrated,
the arrival time receded. We crossed the Rhine,
switched drivers, the children fiddly.
At closest resolution the satnav screen
was featureless, zoom out to see a few
neighbouring roads, further to
the arterials, urban clusters, trunks,
the national circuitry, our island, tilted,
the globe itself. When we got to them
the crashes had moved on. There was
the changing styles of churches.
A pitstop. The long lake was grey and
waterfowl shuffled in mild consternation.
As I unzipped the dusk wafted across
the many-natured rivers, the signs
for the towns we'll never visit. The sky
wore away to reveal the real face.
It was time of the turn of light, stop at a garage
where the coffee had the Ruhr-taste,

anthracite and tar. It is now dark
a passenger in the car in front is death
with a scythe, possibly a rear view mirror.
The last change of driver, the ferry.

The Tunnel

Alongside draws a hearse,
its immaculate insides. The driver
signals to me with both hands,
urgently. Before I can respond
he falls behind. A car tuts. The satnav
is uncertain or contradictory, the kids in
the back refractory, at best.

Approaching Calais, we're
held on the *giratoire*
between HGVs and returnees.
Lines of razorwire,
men paired with Alsatians.
Knurled pebbles by the dunes,
where the road's sentence finds a stop.

The car feels like the car of the sun
once the sun has run its course
but then runs on as needs, unlightened.

It's not that time is short, time is
narrow, you can drive to the end of it
and find you have missed most of what
you thought might hold you back.
Rarely you get the chance to drive it again

as the see through
insect-splatter dazzles.

God Is my Co-Pilot (Flight 4U 9525)

1

I'd only patronise the terrible
open-fronted bookshop in order
to absorb time by the magazine shelves.
See what the latest thinking is
on how fast we are moving from
decline to obliteration. The panelled
bars, saloons, mock. We sit and
watch others eat, then eat and wait out the
delays, then something happens like a girl
skipping or a sparrow lights under the
tables. It is a last call to somewhere
else. A tale telling itself over an
echoless PA system to which
you cannot not listen, even though it
never mentions your flight.
We could move from one table to the next
and call it life. Or stay, and call it the same.

2

Trust the pilot, he rounds the sky.
Explore through him our faith in sides.
The attendants continue to attend,
the transcript of the voices of the pilots
records knocks against the door, the furious
cage that answers gravity shaking.
It is not too late to take charge to
play us out with ropes to
unsafely hold up the ruins of our eyes, assert
the metal strength that held us down, as
holiday strikes on the mountain.
Guts, push them back in, the undamaged arm
holds back its bled form
waves to the climbing party. We go
where stars shear from their earths.

Cigarette Pack

Summer had up to now seemed harmless
but cycling home it is dark, my lights have no batteries
the barriers are being packed away, the festival is over,
a workman waits for me by the gate

something shimmers
towards the feet of the nearby drinkers
it is a cigarette-pack cellophane

one of them grabs me and calls me *dad*
he saw my yellow reflective jacket
more than me, I draw away from him, demurring
but as the lights change I say take care

after-blur of rain-edge on the firm and the infirm

take the road home and take
night to be inside.

Civil Twilight

It is dusk, it is past dusk.
The bigger children use the chance of shadow
to take revenge on the weaker,
parents cluster round a barbecue and
bikes lean under the trees.
At the other side of the park, an
argument progresses musically
and at my end of this rheumy
September I have put myself
in the stocks. I am exhaust
of form, pinioned between
an emptying moon and the plenary
street lights. The exercise machine
shines as I delay the foxes in their
rounds. There are no runners left,
the dogwalkers have been squeezed
out by weight of evening. I can't drain
the iron from structure and watch stars
through trees move difficultly.
The cage is open but the chain catches
in its links. To account
where the dogs pass, to turn
nightly the clock of us back, is work.

How did it get to be so the geese
pull the dark over them? we gather
the little ones in order to leave for home
with the abstract smell of end of evening,

and putting them to bed we hear faint
cries, seeds of cries
from the park, whether of pain or excitement
we could never through trees find.

When a child at night shouts from the street,
you find it hard to place this feeling:
joy, it is named, in its context.

The Lengths

Sensational sweat runs down my spine.
Through the fist-sized mist-hole I make
in the door-window of the Sunday-
afternoon crowded sauna parents
stretch caps onto the heads of children
who cross their arms and tremble
wing-equipped at the pool's lip.
Their caps make them bald and unlovely
until, as the February sun feels for
the submerged floor, they step out—
visible to me in the manner of a frieze—and
into water's insoluble givingness.

Their heads bob, submerge. They speak
in air-cauliflowers, then cling at length's end,
aware they've learnt a language their mothers
forgot. The antenatal group in the deep-end
lean back as one so that their hair spreads
and their weight floats away.

In other lanes the swimmers, turning, meet
their own forms as rising bubbles, and move
through them towards where the low sun
projects onto the non-slip tiles a wavering screen
of blue-green cut-through ripples
and unseen machines replace this water
with more water, piped from the clouds
of months before, and it seems
the rain's purpose in falling was to
construct this moment out of us, sunlight,
and a transparent sense of floating, in
tribute to those of us who remain born.

Commuters

When we drew in, my colleague stood up
—the one I often walk to the office with—
and explained to me that he was not
going to work today. He'd gone blind
he said, in one eye, and needed to see a doctor.
I stepped back in order to look at him
and saw he was not in his work clothes:
a heavy fueillemort sheepskin
over jeans, his eye puffed and dripping.
He looked lonely and scared. I had often
thought of him as one perhaps nearer
to death than me, despite being younger,
due to his poor posture, his limp, his desk
surrounded by wrappers like an autumn
beech-tree. The train door was perfectly
aligned with the station exit. We walked
away in different ways. I waved.

Turd

Ah, lump, is it as I had imagined
down at the post office
large and clearly human on the floor
we conduct our business with stench
and I go to the next shop, where
the same smell malingers.
I slightly suspect this toddler, playing
on the floor. The lump would have
had to work its way down his long trousers

and the mum seems unaware,
so I walk back, my teenager is with his friend
somewhere near, I look in at Costcos to see
their wine rack up
ended, floor running with wine

ah, lump,
under heaven's shadow, frogs mud-wrestle
the apple trees disfruit their rooks
by pedal or motor we recycle
the same routes, return

I cannot type, my face is crumpled and
wrong, we must admit
the space we travel through is intersected
variously by parts that engage
and what falls apart
we must fathom from behind it the agency

ah lump, it all turns on me.

For the Other Artists (for V)

You probably won't remember this but
the barista showed us his tattoo,
an intricately calligraphed couplet
about how compared to a star how small
we are, all of us who walk and see,
and I'm thinking yes, we're
translation-machines, processing
that which is outside us into
scrolls of not-quite text and also we're
forgetting-machines, passing
thoughts into oblivion, as if that's what
we're for. Witness and forget.

But a sentence long-drawn from thought's well
is to the tongue touch: among those who spend
lives realising, it burns inside.
It's not enough to see the half-lit thought
without squeezing from the poor light
the image of a line. Write it as

if we all had one angle
and the fleece clouds
blew from my brain to yours and
then the sand would listen to our
particulars and peel the rocks to show
where, chambered in the fossil record,
blood flows. In the circle of light
from the lightshade a glass stands.
A speck floats: a scale from the wing of
the moth that ascended to heaven by
means of the bulb. Follow its trail,
work it through until morning's standing
wave tricks us back into daylight.

The artists are getting old, we must ask them to
paint exactly, extend, drill their eyes: and
we are all artists. A hired hand turns, an arm
rests, the doctors' shadows surround us.
The brush is in the jar, the canvas is wet.

Assassin's Creed

I am running uphill, it is dark,
even the moon withholds itself.
The animals I see seem too
human, or objects even have an
air of a decision that cannot be made.

Back home I watch my son mass-murder a path
through Istanbul or Constantinople
to the grunts of the dying, leap
alleys over roofs, a screw of tornado-wrath
his hands shaking with light. Head
lit by the screen, saintly hair
highlit and deranged.

It is time to kill him. Perhaps not
today but he must be wakened into
death, real death, shown the way out of
his room. I speak softly, at first
come on now, time for bed.

We made this show of children, their
wavery energy, whatever we do will
influence them, but it is hard to say
how. We float between their
objects, looking at the steps in
front of us, the mud brought in from outside
as if we're sure there is an inside.

I'll kill him with insight. With Freud.
It's time to put away your toys:
there are further and colder things that with hard
work and no sleep can also be destroyed.

Mahmud

Mahmud, you leaf, falling, on the street,
image after image, world before and behind
photographer of tree-bark, boulevardier,
stick walker, emperor of notes: death
pursues you leadenly to tell you:
all are equal among the millings,
the afterlife masses, offcut, infected.
Take nothing for the journey. Misty
dimness, darkness before the eyes.
You tell me Jesus was lucky to die young,
a few hours on the cross was nothing to
age. Jesus should have grown old, that would
have been, you say, sufficient suffering.

You spoke of decay, of day-breath, the drawn light.
I have this thing where when I hear
of an impending death, I bristle with anticipation
and when the news comes I feel a beat
of happiness. I refer you to my
growing up with a terminal father
interminably crawling to the toilet
at 2 am, apologising, then vomiting
loudly. Let it be over I think, it must come
soon. Then the guilt, hours or days later
the grief. But no Mahmud, how can I
want you back in your cold wifeless house
which we can't visit. Instead
I cycle past the hospital, its brutal collapsed
trilithon set against Brunel's tree-clad viaduct.
I cycle down to the Thames.
It is high and fast. A woman shakes
out a bag of crumbs and is surrounded
by the accusative bladed gulls.
But how can I write this in a poem, Mahmud?
Love's complexity shown in a flock lifting
as one, as I drive my bike through them

back towards the hospital,
pause at the apex of the steep-arched bridge
and look back: the ducks have made circles
in the suddenly still water, but by the time my phone is out
the wind has ruffled these to nothing, there is
nothing to photograph, I am not thinking at all
about you Mahmud, only later, flicking through
my camera roll there's the photo I did not take,
the kingfisher, the lost instant streaking
the eye's field, particle of rainbow,
dislodged joy, bird of grief.

Snowfield

Our boots maraud into that fresh
first void. Last spring
had been made less meaningful
by that winter's lack of snow;
but absence is now its memory
as the children scuff grey
fireworks on the pavement
and roll balls into unlimbed figures
into men. Coming from the bath,
that evening, their china skins
still feel cold. Later, in darkness, I run
the hardened parks of West London
and a dog tracks among meadows
where loss is a sentence moving
towards but never reaching its
completion. The men standing into
the dusk are sinking in. They call to me
and the dirt is visible
inside them. I also am
one of those the children made.

Rain

Landlord of sea, sky
your hooved beats on hard mud
knock the faces off the dead.
It is morning and seldom so wet
a sift, a balance in the hours.

I have to drive through this to
get to the place
from which I shall be able to head out.

Lightning's ziggurat is all side, angle.

Query the leaf, tremble that palm,
come home to find a new poem.
Set off in a ship of fools for far shores,
seek for the kings of nothing.
It is a day of song, I peer into my diary's
incontinent sky

flowers shake open like the rain of the night before
pondweed reconfigures
a butterfly wing
unhinges.

From the willow
parentheses float down the river.

Meet my syntax: a municipal
moon pondering against
the rising invisible stars.

Return Train

Winter's chemotherapy has thinned the local parks
and in the valley, the many-natured river
and all of the named fragments that are people
take their ghosts with them, colonies of ghosts.

I sit on a fold-down and watch
a woman in front of me watch
on her screen an actor fire.
War leaks in to the carriage, and sentences
from the free newspaper form columns.
Hurt them by looking. Saw through
the investment arms. Spectres
in the aisle laugh between us, devices
overflow: phones, papers, arms.

Push down the sun.
Rust's slow fire spreads, silts fan across.
Believe the clouds, when darkening.
Lights form buildings. We tire but have to sit
as if to attention. Some trees brush past.
The point arrives when there is no
difference between cloud, sky, and horizon.
This is the point of indefinition, where
our unworkable assumption buckles.
Turn of the day, return of the worker.

An unanswered phone. Opposite me,
a man cries, silently, openly.

Heat

The hewn clouds spill dust.
God drives his war-car
of smoke, brimstone and creak,
pursuing the sun until his helmet
melts. He melts. Surely he can
outface it, but as he descends his train
stalls, warps, he liquefies, cries.

This that catches in his throat is language.
The wind stops breathing,
flame parts the living from the gross.
I woke crying to find the window
open, storm had appeared in us,
the breath spoke out of turn

which does not explain how I keep rising
with a bicycle clip around my ankle, as if
in sleep I'd continued cycling

as each plane faded
like a raindrop on brick.

The Living

Pale winter light slants into the beech-wood
and upon the disembodied rooves
as we carry the living down into our rooms.
They pick themselves from the floor
and smoke from every mouth. Spirit
pours out of them as they sit
among us and stir in the blue hour what
they think is their tea. They do not see
us among whom they are visitors
in their own houses: the cold draft,
the cracks in their crockery, sudden
interruption to connectivity.

Arranged like eyelets, nights thread us.
We have the impression that the carpet gives.
A moth staggers from a wall and standing

they confuse their steps with ours,
inhabit our shadows, our prints.
The kettle's steam is ours, the flies
on the laptop, wringing their hands, are also
us. The living are wringing our hands.

The Hard Problem

The head abuts on the hard problem
the matter of thought. Waking once
when ill it seemed clear I was
also the bed, the ward. But
I lifted my head and these spilt
out. Spots of me on the pillow
or just shadow.

The get-well-soon balloon trailed
its umbilical, followed visitors'
backdraughts, butted the door.
Something that language does to you
to do with language. The head
carried out the body out of the room.

At the lake I took the image as
preferable, since contingent on
leaf-fall, wind-scuff or fish-pucker, to
the actual trees. The surface shot back
what I don't know. I was wobbled,
mirrors cracked in me and in place of mind

to have what, spirit of pronoun. Growing
in amethyst caves not much more than fist-
sized, the brain that science sees cannot see
its litness, screens in each cell waking.

We clean them by sleeping, these cells, knowing
how flowed it is in us, vat of brain that
tilts, spills sentence, and comes again,
animates, feels a way, senses

self as a head that extrudes from the eye,
as if towards light, pushing, hardening.

Partial Eclipse

Eclipse! N miscalled you
apocalypse, I think of this standing
outside the bank, folding
the notes into my wallet, the day's
healed counterfact, and still the awkward
silent beeches ignite with pigeons
pushing against a refreshed breeze,
odd shiver through these streets
as the feel of a slight fever when tired,
from which there may be a normal to
return to as through a glass door.
A twilight with shadows. In
the office it is as if none of this
happened, as indeed it did not,
a horned portent fading in my eye.

The Tower

The tower is visible from hills away
though in late summer
it's hard to tell which turn to take.
Cats drowse on warm gravel.
A child with a stick stirs
three goats out of our way.
Our road briefly parallels a stone road
with a green centre, cart or mule track.
Sometimes walled, flower-filled,
losing itself as it turns. Then
the tower is above us.
I park beside an under-construction
hotel. Diggers pile rubble.
A new storm bruises the sky.

An old foot-track strings into
a cricket-loud meadow and on through woods.
The ways are unincluded,
clouded or occluded, thickly treed,
where the limbs turn unusually, then
from the clumped gloom, walls
just low enough for us to scale:
the kids ahead of me, I catch
snatches of them through
undergrowth. Then silence, splenetic
rubble. A caretaker with a barrow
nods us over a plank-bridge.
The security fence sings.
My old bike-light with the broken
bracket emits a half light. We feel
a presence buzz, and our limbs
are agitated from above.

We emerge into rain,
arranged in order of breath.
The song lets down its string,
the rising invisible stars throb
above a throughout blackness.

When I view the pictures later they are
blurry, a leg or foot, a child's arm
sinks into masonry.

Thames Walk

Step onto the dark-worn footpath. The Thames
weeps slowly into London, then sweeps back,
the children peer at water's appearance
as light lightens the lengthening grass.
N. periodically stops walking.
Cyclists tink their bells and gulls
scatter. S. tells me about golems (saying
'gollums'), then says he'd been in a race
with millions and won, and I was curious
he saw his self in the sperm, not the more
massive egg. As did I. We note,
on a half-sunk narrow-boat, the heron's
holding stare. A sign tells us 'this
footpath closes at dusk'. It's dusk, we
take it, between tall hedges and heavy-
barked trees. N. already has that way
of taking an arm. The river slops in
the tree, light laces through. The squirrels move
away from us by the length by which for
them the world is eased.

Here comes the swan: a popemobile
through a crowd of ducks. People hold pints
and phones, suddenly separately
shouting: a goal had been scored in Russia
but what we notice is the girl in
the mud, her intense regard towards the ebb:
a withdrawn plane and the ribs of what is
under and her mother calling softly
to her to come back, and the name
she calls is Scheherazade.

Third Child

From the recreation-centre café
I look out over a high room, sectioned
into badminton and other courts, at
the far end of which, partly behind
a screen, S in a *judogi*
wrestles with a girl, as somewhere else
a woman makes echoey cries of effort.

Driving home, the mistuned radio scrapes
as if the singer in singing
disembodied the song. I go on extended
runs, the canals by night, or dawn,
past long factories that smell of made
dinners and Indian sweets, watch
waterbirds loosening the sun, landing in
unison. It is then I think of the divisible

near-child of always-morning, branching
almost-arms, compound of eyes
and language, embryon of text. I try
to remove from him the implied
lip print on air, imagine the boy who
never stranded his head in the adult bed,
folded to the neck against the cold
some sludge of waking
warns us how in this we should seek
the real children hatched between limbs.

The child we did not in the end
have. We approach his road but cannot
see him, and the soft floor is where we fall.

Infinity Pool, Snowdonia

Dreamt I was a shadow of myself, in
the same job, but hardly able to function.
All screen, I was halfway to sleep
when Z whispered my name and I said,
I am so tired, and she left what she was
saying, but from then I could not shake
free from the chains of work.
It is always dark in this kind of dream, until
I break through, then I am
at the pool again, half way
up the Watkins Path in full sun with N,
the fluent water of Afon Cum Llan
screws its surfaces, light's tortuosity
rills across granite and the bathers
take selfies with a backdrop of the rest of Wales:
sky's curvature, unshorn idling clouds.

Does anyone complain that the world is
too full of forms, crowdedly crying, and the forms
and the birds wear thin before
the sound of the river making love.
A hand floats before the idea of rain.
A gang of swallows picks off mosquitoes.

More likely form is what we construct
to stop us falling into the earth.

The Slug at the Door

The infant nail is spurt of
future. Wheels in the eye turn;
a crack opens in him
like a tunnel in a hand.

Breach is breath, to breathe we breach.
Sunlight breaks down in the rose.
A tremble, a petal falls.
The light moves a moment from its image.
Moon abuts realms of felt clouds, clawed
thoughts restate mind over master.
We come down in tether,
mist proceeds when the weather turns.

We have stone colds, continue
to not understand each other. Thought
severs selves and grinds shapes out of skin:

these are the curves of what-is,
the flow-finding of the making impulse
telling us there is no in in infinite. To observe
the bubble-beaded glass
raise it from the table: here's to
everything that is not us.
Slugs answer with their bodies:
a foot in the door, a toe-hold,

and as the wind throws up its leaves
spirit moves in it, and
music surrounds us.

Acknowledgments

Anger: *Events* (Canada)
Coal: *Poetry Wales*
Excess: *Havik*
For the Other Artists: *Cathexis*
Gravity: *Wild Word*
Heron Ascending: *Wild Word*
Horse: *Tishman Review*
Košava: *Tiny Seed*
No Ideas: *Inverted Syntax*
Partial Eclipse: *Osiris*
Quoth the Sea: *Inverted Syntax*
Rain: *Southern Humanities Review*
Thames Walk: *Roanoke Review*
The Day of the Drive: *Michigan Quarterly Review*
The Language: *Riddled with Arrows*
The Wren: *Tiny Spoon*
Third Child: Southampton Review
Train poems: earlier versions appeared in *Season Tickets* (Periplum, 2019)

About the Author

Giles Goodland grew up in the rural west of England and now lives in West London. He has worked as a researcher and then an editor of the *Oxford English Dictionary*. He has published numerous papers on early modern literature and language, and now lectures for Oxford University's Department of Continuing Education. His poetry books include *Littoral* (Oversteps, Devon, 1996), *A Spy in the House of Years* (Leviathan, 2001), *Capital* (Salt, Cambridge, 2006), *What the Things Sang* (Shearsman, Exeter, 2009), *The Dumb Messengers* (Salt, 2012), *Gloss* (Knives Forks and Spoons, Manchester, 2016), *The Masses* (Shearsman, 2018).

Author photo by Nina Goodland.
Used by permission.

Free Verse Editions

Edited by Jon Thompson

13 ways of happily by Emily Carr
& in Open, Marvel by Felicia Zamora
Alias by Eric Pankey
Ariadne, A Series by Martha Ronk
At Your Feet (A Teus Pés) by Ana Cristina César, edited by Katrina Dodson, trans. by Brenda Hillman and Helen Hillman
Bari's Love Song by Kang Eun-Gyo, translated by Chung Eun-Gwi
Between the Twilight and the Sky by Jennie Neighbors
Blood Orbits by Ger Killeen
The Bodies by Christopher Sindt
The Book of Isaac by Aidan Semmens
The Calling by Bruce Bond
Canticle of the Night Path by Jennifer Atkinson
Child in the Road by Cindy Savett
Civil Twilight by Giles Goodland
Condominium of the Flesh by Valerio Magrelli, trans. by Clarissa Botsford
Contrapuntal by Christopher Kondrich
Country Album by James Capozzi
Cry Baby Mystic by Daniel Tiffany
The Curiosities by Brittany Perham
Current by Lisa Fishman
Day In, Day Out by Simon Smith
Dear Reader by Bruce Bond
Dismantling the Angel by Eric Pankey
Divination Machine by F. Daniel Rzicznek
Elsewhere, That Small by Monica Berlin
Empire by Tracy Zeman
Erros by Morgan Lucas Schuldt
Fifteen Seconds without Sorrow by Shim Bo-Seon, trans. by Chung Eun-Gwi and Brother Anthony of Taizé
The Forever Notes by Ethel Rackin
The Flying House by Dawn-Michelle Baude
Ghost Letters by Baba Badji
Go On by Ethel Rackin
Here City by Rick Snyder
Instances: Selected Poems by Jeongrye Choi, trans. by Brenda Hillman, Wayne de Fremery, & Jeongrye Choi
Last Morning by Simon Smith

The Magnetic Brackets by Jesús Losada, trans. by M. Smith & L. Ingelmo
Man Praying by Donald Platt
A Map of Faring by Peter Riley
The Miraculous Courageous by Josh Booton
Mirrorforms by Peter Kline
No Shape Bends the River So Long by Monica Berlin & Beth Marzoni
North | Rock | Edge by Susan Tichy
Not into the Blossoms and Not into the Air by Elizabeth Jacobson
Overyellow, by Nicolas Pesquès, translated by Cole Swensen
Parallel Resting Places by Laura Wetherington
Physis by Nicolas Pesquès, translated by Cole Swensen
Pilgrimage Suites by Derek Gromadzki
Pilgrimly by Siobhán Scarry
Poems from above the Hill & Selected Work by Ashur Etwebi, trans. by Brenda Hillman & Diallah Haidar
The Prison Poems by Miguel Hernández, trans. by Michael Smith
Puppet Wardrobe by Daniel Tiffany
Quarry by Carolyn Guinzio
remanence by Boyer Rickel
Republic of Song by Kelvin Corcoran
Rumor by Elizabeth Robinson
Settlers by F. Daniel Rzicznek
Signs Following by Ger Killeen
Small Sillion by Joshua McKinney
Split the Crow by Sarah Sousa
Spine by Carolyn Guinzio
Spool by Matthew Cooperman
Strange Antlers by Richard Jarrette
Summoned by Guillevic, trans. by Monique Chefdor & Stella Harvey
Sunshine Wound by L. S. Klatt
System and Population by Christopher Sindt
These Beautiful Limits by Thomas Lisk
They Who Saw the Deep by Geraldine Monk
The Thinking Eye by Jennifer Atkinson
This History That Just Happened by Hannah Craig
An Unchanging Blue: Selected Poems 1962–1975 by Rolf Dieter Brinkmann, trans. by Mark Terrill
Under the Quick by Molly Bendall
Verge by Morgan Lucas Schuldt
The Visible Woman by Allison Funk
The Wash by Adam Clay

We'll See by Georges Godeau, trans. by Kathleen McGookey
What Stillness Illuminated by Yermiyahu Ahron Taub
Winter Journey [Viaggio d'inverno] by Attilio Bertolucci, trans. by Nicholas Benson
Wonder Rooms by Allison Funk

www.ingramcontent.com/pod-product-compliance
Ingram Content Group UK Ltd.
Pitfield, Milton Keynes, MK11 3LW, UK
UKHW041642190726
13854UKWH00006B/2645